Joy C Green

Words of Joy

pictures, idioms, stories, songs and poems

©greenvoices/2022
4th edition

Herausgeber: Institut Green Voices

Verantwortlich: Joy C. Green

@2022

Herstellung und Verlag:

BoD - Books on Demand, Norderstedt

ISBN : 9783756844098

Impressum:
Joy C. Green
Institut Green Voices
Felicitas- Fuess- Str 13
81827 München

info@greenvoices.de

Mobil: 0178-6028526

Joy C Green

Words
of
Joy

pictures, idioms, stories, songs and poems

1st edition
published july 2007
by
www.greenvoices.de
Copyright, 2007,
by Joy C. Green Munich, Germany

Introduction

The communication between us has come to a frightening staleness.
I would like to refresh and enrich your life with a few positive impressions and encourage your thinking about your personal situation for a minute.
All of our lifes are filled with amazing opportunities, only have we to develop the yearn to discover them
May this little book give you some positive, thoughtful and awakening moments.
I want to dedicate this book to my inspirations:
Dennis
Jennifer
Tamiko Nova
Phyllis
Alvin
and my past
A special thank you
to my three wonderful daughters,
my son and Garance who contributed some of the included painting artifacts.
And to Simon Schott who discovered our art abilities.
with all my love

JOY

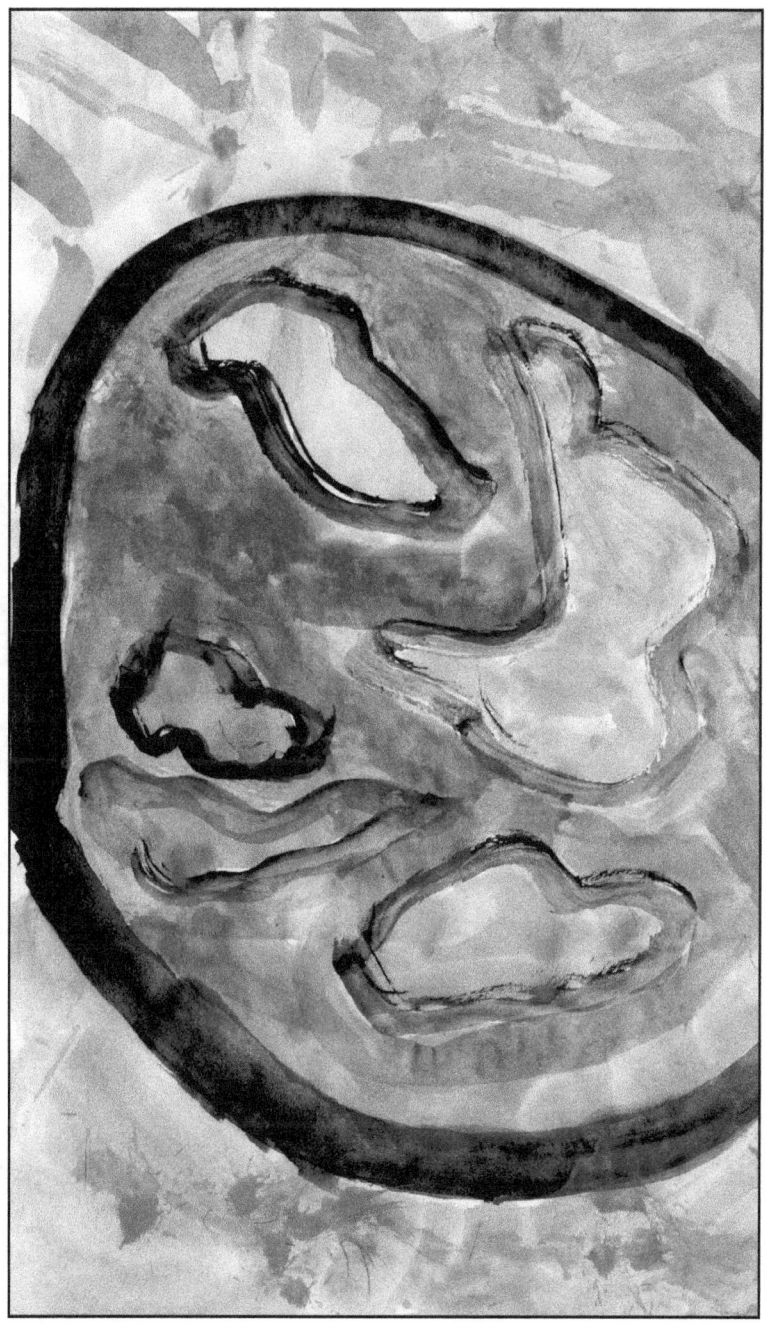

About

Life

The Earth

my color is yellow
my warmth gives you confidence and comfort
my soil feeds your hunger and inflames your
desire
my peace eases your fears
my arms embrace you with love and protect you
my silence answers your doubts,
rests your storms
and quiet your yells
my wisdom drys your tears and tells the future
my wholeness gives you freedom
I am the foundation and the meaning of your life
I am
your mother earth

sep, 2005

The Fire

my color is red
my vehemency gives you eloquence
my impatience is your liveliness
my unrestrainity breaks down your limitations
my unpredictability inflames new experiments
my flame is your ignition
my heat is your desire and your sexuality
my fascination arises your curiousity
out of my vigor deceased reerect
I am your warmth, your power and your fertility
I am your sister
fire

oct 3rd,2005

Friendship

pitt'n , patt'n, pout'n, puuhh
one, two, three and out are you
do you have what it takes or not
can I gain or have I got

children jugde the way we teach them
we determine what we live
nobody is as bad as we are
it's a game of take and give

friendship
second word that's been misused for ages
like love

only heard one good definition of friendship:
„ Friendship is to love and respect the others
work and life and take interest in it."
(thank you Alex)

Pastina, aug 10th, 2005

Hot Summer City
(in memory of summer 1990 and my family down south)

Big wheels dressed up in the night of the city
girls on the corner so cool and so pretty
streets full of people, the sweat in the air
breathe in the life and the fear, the despair

Dont know where they going,
ride their boredom away
they keep on ridin' til the break of the day

HOT SUMMER night in a hot summer city
life in the fast lane leaves no time for pity

He's turning the wheel, she's earning the bills
he's got the money so she follows his will
if you've got nothin, there's nothin to loose
they dont see the lies that they decided to choose

Dont know where they going, ride their anger away
they keep on ridin' til the break of the day

(soundtrack, aug 1992)

„...the illusory certainties of the old are no more....and only Inner Knowing can replace them in this world without direction.."

Indian wisdom
Grandfather Little Crow, USA

Let me be- me

One voice in a crowd of voices
screaming, yelling silently
trying not to fight the other
opposing very quietly

can't endure the tragic structure
people call the facts of life
find no sense in hollow scenics
try to ease the stress and jive

watch the pain they cause with words,
wasted energy of mind
wonder why the simple answers
can't be found in being kind

love and respect don't seem to be
of any higher value and not worth
to be considered an solution
instead one choose the witches curse

war in everybodies kitchen
seem to be the common choice
and fading in the noise of warfare
is the one opposing voice
although there is a yearn for changes
yet not to be found in thee"
my answer for the peace and freedom
can only be: let me be- me

april 2nd, 1999

Little Things

It's not the 20.000 $ juwel
or the dinner at the RITZ
neither the Louis XIV stool
or being on TV with FRITZ !
seen the show offs much to often
never did they hit my spot
hate when you can't show you're simple too
just care of all the things you've got

I'm sure there are a million people
whose aim in life is just like yours
but that's not me
not me
and it will never be
never be me

it was the shy touch of my chin
and your shyness deep within
that made me fall
in love with you
gave me the call
to love you too

it were the dimples in your face
the glance that longed for my embrace
that made me fall
into your arms
that let me fall
for all your warmth

your lips that show your whole mind
your hands that love to be kind
that made me fall
in love with you
over and over
cause that is true

It's not the 20.000 $ juwel
or dinner at a fancy place
it is not anybody elses rule
or anyhow the matter of your race !

I hope there are a million people who might think
the way I do
cause that is me
and it will always be
me hoping
love will set us free

nov 21st, 1998

Magic
(for my mom)
1. There are moments full of worries
how much longer You'll be here with me
and I feel disturbed and sorry
for each single time we disagree
2. When I see your face I think it's mine
when I hear your voice, it's all so kind
you tought me the values of my life
to see you going cuts me like a knife
and when I look into your eyes
There's magic
how you face tomorrow
and it gives me hope and strenghth to carry on
it's magic
how you fight your sorrow
and it gives me reason to be strong
3. I remember well how I drove you mad
by the many funny friends I had
never learned enough for school and then
went to parties danced until the morning came
4. Everybody tries to be the perfect mom or child
but we're humans some are mean and wild
when my daughter's old enough to understand
I will tell her of the greatest mom I had
and when I look into your eyes
There's magic... !
I wonder why is life that way,
and I'm running out of things to say

(soundtrack, recorded on 13th june 1993, the day my mom died)

The Metal

my color is white
I carry all other colors within me
my rigidity holds your life frame
my variety enlightens your life with wonders
my clearness opens new rooms
my strictness liberates new options
my architecture stabilizes your lifes' construction
my narrowness is your freedom
I am the basis and the structure of your life
I am
the grandfather metal

sep 2005

Perfection

Her hair full, blond and naturally curled
a teeny smile with full and lustful lips
a body styled for modelling around the world
a personality so suitable for TV clips
determined and so easy going
and then
her voice so thin and tiny- years of sweat to come
to eventually become strong enough to work !

A t-shirt extra large and pants in double size
yet still too tight to fit
a hairdresser would win an extra prize
to help a little bit
a face you wouldnt chose to go to dinner with
and then
a voice so brillant, strong and perfect
you'd melt away like ice cream on a summer day

He had the rebel look in all his moves
tall, skiny and a jaw rejecting questions yet unasked
born for stage with all its proofs
his ways all natural and so unmasked
his voice all clear and so determined
and then
the woman of his dreams convinced him
a decent classic job would please her more

A sense of humor that would beat all known
looks decent and a face of brightest minds
eyes all expressions and up- grown
a voice that gives you chills all kinds
so full of warmth and feeling
and then
there's nothing else in life that scares her more
than stage

Four out of hundreds astonishing examples
- all happened here befor my eyes
the daily mess with talent and genetics,
moods, education and lifes' strife

One of a million will have a better balance
of skills and looks, support and serious emotion
a million hours work will do the rest to talents
on the everlasting way through their devotion

to perfection

dec 26th, 2003

The Schemer
(to my brother)

Just midnight- you get me out of bed
complain your day was a mess
and that your body is aching in pain
- I think I couldnt care less
And while you're seeking for mercy
you're pushing it too far
you're telling meaningless tales
I'm all fed up with these numerous games
this time my pity just fails
You're a schemer with no obstructions
you're a dazzler beg for advice
you're playin with my heart
your aim's destruction
don't you know it's your turn to pay the price
You're a schemer with no restrictions
you're a dazzler look for device
you're playing with my heart with contradictions
Listen, now I've learnt you've been telling lies !
Friday evening- you call me up again
say you cant sleep anymore
that you've been wasting all week in despair
to find what you're living for
then you bother, annoy me through hours on the phone
all questions end with denies
and you behave like an unpleasant child
that keep on telling me lies !
WHY- just why- why don't you- go leave me alone

(soundtrack, may 1993)

Solitude

turning and a spinning
seems no matter where I go
I cant loose for winning
cant accept a masceraded no

all these million phases
dancing in my head
opening new cases
funny, crazy, mad
masks behind odd features
fear to loose my mind
in these senseless creatures
troubles cant unwind
every second new sensations
visions through the nights
in ongoing motivation
passions, fears and fights
plans and golden aims
dares to dream and win
endless routes for games
ideas just begin
only few companions
friends along the way
matching disillusions
taking solitude away

jan 6th, 2004 march 23rd, 2005

Symphony of Life

Every breeze
passing by your face
every sun beam
with its sweet embrace
every thunder
breaking into silence
leaves that fall and play
smoothing down the violence

Every blossom
sweetening the air
every birds song
talking of despair
every rain drop
pattering the pasture
every lightning
flashing the desaster
Every move in life
every single strife
every twinkle of your eye
every bid fare-well, good-bye
every minute you inhale
moments tasting stale
all is but a melody
to life
everything's a tone
blue or bright
heavy or light
everything a part of
the big symphony of life

dec 24th, 2003

The Water

my color is blue
my depth calms your soul
my purity clears your minds
my consistency lifts all weight
my existence is your existence
my energy is your power
my stream and flow is never ending
I evolve from the earth
I am the beginning and the end
I am
the water

sep 2005

The Wood

my color is green
my seed is the beginning of your dream
my impatience is the constructor of your desires
my unperturbance is the guarantee for your
success
my endurance leads your strength
my flexibility allows all your visions to flow
my curiousity is your enlightment
my branches will reach into infinity
I am the basis and the existence of your life
I am
your father wood

sep 2005

About

Love

As Long As I Have You

dreams of passion
dreams of tenderness
I don't have to dream no more

longing for the look
of understanding love
I don't have to look no more

fears of pain and heartaches
threats of future games
I don't have to fear no more

flew into my life
angel like
from heaven sent
fly back into my arms tonight
and hold me
warm and tender

and I know
I don't need anybody else
as long as I have you

aug 22th, 1998

Don't
don't ever walk passed me
without looking into my eyes

don't ever wake up in the morning
without the yearn to hold me for a moment

don't let us sit on a bench one day
not knowing what to say

don't ever look at me
without the glow of love in your eyes

don't ever stop
to miss my touch

don't ever worry
to speak your mind

don't ever let our time together
-every minute, every day-become
indifferent

don't ever let us cease
to work on happiness and love

just don't

jan 31st, 1999

Fly
(to all the lovers)
I smell your perfume on my skin
love that fills me deep within
I cant wait to feel your lips on me again tonight
holding me last night
your body laid so close and tight
I cant wait to feel your love surrounding me tonight

You know how to excite me
my heart beats out of time
my body shakes, resistance breaks and
I feel you are mine !
Your eyes give off that certain glow
need no words cause I just know
your love for me will always be so far beyond all words
I WANNA FLY - SO HIGH !
No matter if you're far or near
I'll be never scared with fear
'cause I'm aware that you'll be there
your love will make me strong
I dont care what people say
they just envy anyway
when love is real and when we feel
we know where we belong
You know how to excite me
my heart beats out of time
my body shakes, resistance breaks
and I feel you are mine
When our time is meant to be
our love will set us free
and I am sure there's gonna be
a place for you and me
(nov, 1993)- soundtrack

Just Love

Never thought it could be
so easy
to feel like butterflies
to tremble out of pure excitement
and anticipation
for the lovers hands
to breathe the scent of passion
with every breath you take
to love the pain
of longing
cause it is not in vain

Yes, it can be so easy
not to hurt
each other
when there is nothing
to proove
cause we simply love
to be in love

july 28th, 1998

Keep on Going
(dedicated to Elbert)

Yes, you know its all shook up
your life got out of track, you see its bad
you find no way to change or stop
the mess around you that makes you mad

There're always two sides to a coin
I'll pick the one that tells me ‚go and fight'
you have to get in gear- keep goingand
dont slide on the other side

Where you'll go, remember all my words

Keep on going- just keep on
no matter if your heart's in pain
just keep on- keep on going
may destiny recall your name

You're damn' aware there should be more
than freezing lonesome in the cold of life,
but you know things worth fighting for
to keep your aims and dreams alive

Yes, you know it's all shook up,
it's up to you to win or loose it;
you have to strain back up on top
'cause that's the way you should be choosin'

(soundtrack, 1993)

Miss

Sunshine in the early morning
sunshine every night with me
I can see in every movement
all the care you feel for me

Without words an understanding
thoughts so closely known to me
glances full of heart and passion
tenderness that sets me free
And it seems that I can't ask for anything more
and then I wonder :

do I miss..
the nights of hatred
do I miss
the fights for love
do I miss
the pain of dissapointment
and the praying,
tears for love

Open heart with growing feeling
devils from the past disperse
catch me everytime I'm falling
and my woman-kind emerse

and I know
that I dont have to ask for anything more
dec 23rd, 1998

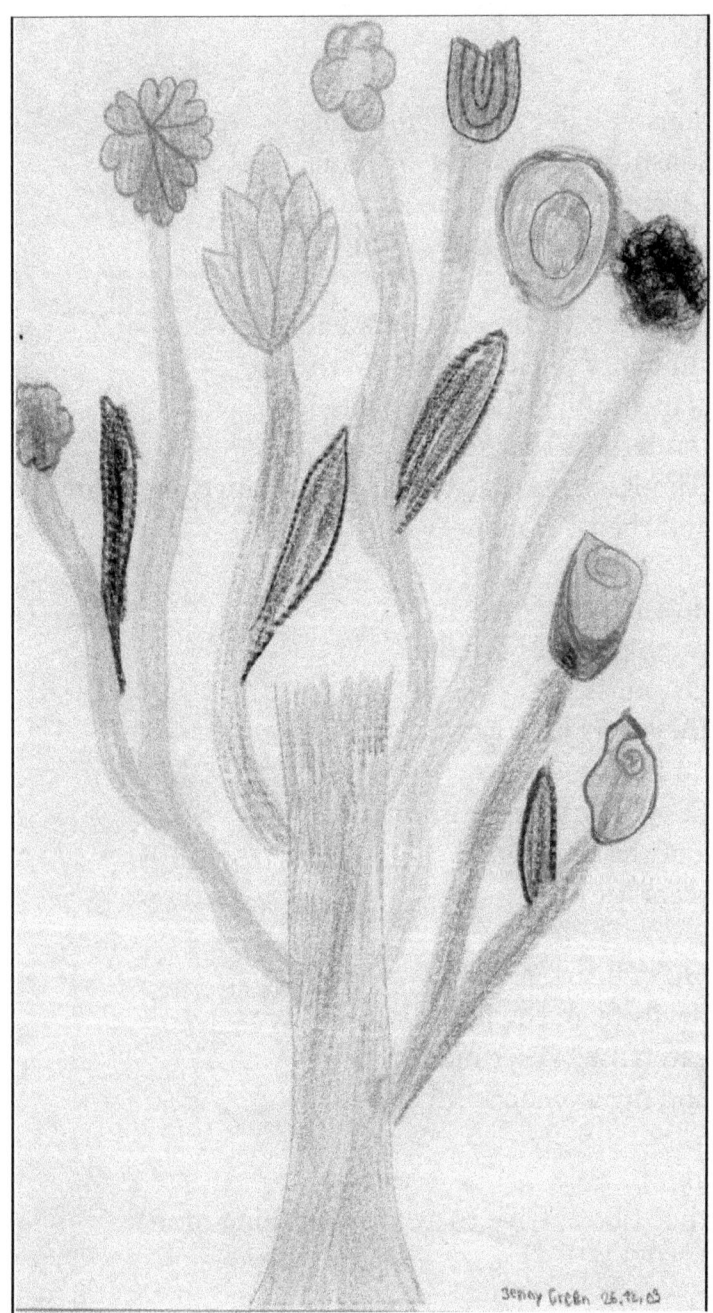

No Love to Give

1. There might not be a thunderstorm
and yet there's heavy rain
there might not be a baby born
and yet there's heavy strain
2. There might have been a hundred friends
and yet you felt alone
there might have been a wonderland
yet, no place to come home
You can travel you can work, you can have it all
.. if you don't have no love to give
you gonna loose it all
3. There might have been the longest night
and yet no sleep did come
there might have been a hundred lights
yet no place you belong
4. There might have been the longest talk
and yet no word was said
there might have been the sweetest walks,
yet filled with deepest regrets
You can travel you can work, you can have it all
.. if you don't have no love to give
you gonna loose it all
If you can't give love, if you can't give love
you don't have love at all
If you can't give love, if you can't give love
you don't own love at all

(soundtrack, june, 1993)

The Power of Love

never has there been one word
as often used and misused as this one
mingled, squeezed and left unknown
to the most quite an adventure

centuries have passed with tons of
books and poems, lyrics and descriptions
all these words have not concretely
shown the matter of the issue

by chance or intentionally
the confusion seems to have been planned
for amusement of the youngsters
for the smiles of wisdom of the olds

have you found the riddles clue?
are you fighting with the matter?
have you balanced the confusion?
are you still a victim of lifes' process?

while the question is still lingering
and never might it find its reply
take a quiet look inside to what
is keeping you alive and why
there the curtain draws to finalize the act
and the answer becomes real
nothing fills your life with strength
like the power of your love

dec 25th, 2003

Touch

If you just knew how much
a single touch
can mean

it can ease your pain
it can heal your wounds

it can caress your soul
it can excite your body

it can wipe your tears away
it can warm your heart

it can relax your stress
it can ease your mind

it can refill your energy
it can receive life
it can hold your love

all that
with just
one touch
that's filled
with honest
emotion

nov 21st, 1998

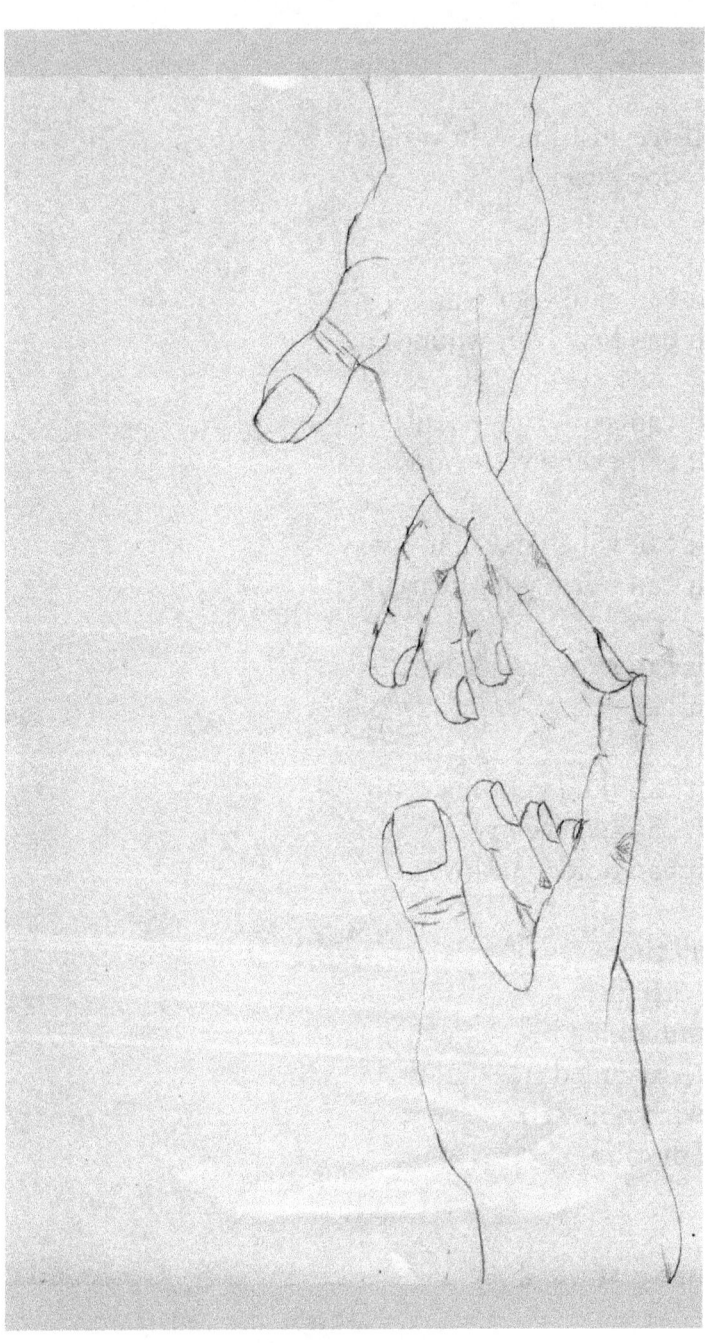

Sometimes
(to André, who keeps me going)

The road was long,-the road was stoney
and trouble seemed to be your name
some days of joy, some days just lonely
while life kept changing like a game
any place you went was just an interlude
you're moving on-andyou
can't deny you're aching for a place
where you belong
- got to go on !
Sometimes you have to break away
although it feels so wrong
sometimes you have to cut your heart
to make it grow back strong
Sometimes it takes more strength and will
more courage than you find
sometimes it seems to be no way
to leave the past behind
All through the time you kept on going
so many people crossed your life
a way to learn, a way of showing
that it takes courage to survive
Had so many times you felt like staying here
but had to move onyou
learn to see that pain is part of life
and growing strong
- got to grow strong !

(soundtrack, 1993)

Would You Mind

Would you mind
if I told you
that your smile means more to me
right know
then all the things you could tell me
Would you mind
if I just held you
without words and promises
and filled my heart
with the smell of your being
Would you mind
if I did play a childish game with you
instead of being serious
so I can feel
you all over next to me
Would you mind
if I just caressed you all night
without the flame of passion
so I fcel save and sound
like a baby in need
Would you mind
if I preferred the feel
of closeness and tenderness
tonight
and snuggle
into my emotions
like into a blanket
of love

nov 21st, 1998

Your Lips

Your lips open my heart
your embrace
opens my mind
your tenderness gives back my hope for truth

your desire purifies
my body from abuse

your love encourages my mind
to fly into beautiful dimensions

your lust opens a world of colors
inside my body
your thoughts give me the trust
into my aims

you are a world within my world

(soundtrack, july 1997)

(music from Marc M. Batschkus)

About

Hope & Future

The Best Years of my Life

photographs and memories linger in my mind
pictures of unbounded laughter with our worries far behind
eyes of undiscovered truths, sticky fingers in my face
little teardrops on my t-shirt and a snuggling embrace
dirty nails and unbrushed hair, missing socks and panty hose
switching dresses with big sisters, chocolate smile and running nose
stones and bears on pillow cases, treasures of a million beads
fightings over cookie crumbs, drawings on my music sheets
toothpaste in the kitchen sink, sugar crunchies in my bed
on my arm an ink pen heart and at night a little head
undivided concentration, spider legs and cricket wings,
cracks in stones and glass in sunlight, morning birdy sings
those were times we cannot measure
our happiness in scales
through the nights and days we carry
energy with endless tales
living life in all its fullness
never stopping in its strive
leaves no time for bitter feelings
in the best years of our life

pastina, italy, august 22nd 2005

Circle of Searching

wrinkled dollar bills on an old set list
last good-bye and stale taste in my mouth
driving home through early morning mist
3am and heading south

few reflections of the moon in puddles
faces, moments, laughes and cries
intertwining mem'ry huddles
resuming in returning whys

is that all that's left and does it matter ?
should I have foreseen the course ?
could I've changed the ways for better ?
would I've battled with the force ?

10 years later knowing more
learned a lot and lost some dreams
keep on searching,- yeah, what for ?
it'll come to me- it seems

pastina, aug 2005
(The Funny Valentines, march 1996- july 2005)

Destination

running, searching, desperate thinking
floating in lethargy
we keep measuring our living
in diplomas colorf'lly

as I grew up - recently
I was told
that generally
we have options manyfold

from the day we start on living
we can find our destiny
in the meanings and in listening
to the elders history

in the understanding of it all
we will realize that we
are not the ones to choose
but to accept it finally

pastina, aug 10th 2005

Distinction

corset of distinction
who has heard of such a thing?
I did
now
I can find no rest.
astonishing how one thing
leads right into another
created one vision
secretly smiled about it,
jugded it as too childish,- first
and thenstarted
to have a dream,
the dream became a plan,
all of a sudden-- real
right along
follows more then just
another vision
there are plans
one right after another
they all become reality
you wait to fail
but still can't stop to dream
while you create
another reality
astonishing how one thing
leads right into another
there seems to be
no time to rest

feb 7th, 2004

Von Tami Für Joy

7.3.05

Freedom

Freedom in a land of glory
freedom in despair and pain
brutality, abuse and madness
and there is nothing left to gain

Freedom that became a phrase
for most people know no shame
hollow words for hollow images
every war a materialistic game

Freedom in a world of glory
freedom for the wealthy guys
all the others left to struggle
with the worries for their lifes

Freedom in this world of tragic
freedom where there seems no hope
folks that can't voice their opinion
lifes hang on a silky rope

Freedom in this world for life
freedom in your hearts and souls
through our courage and our strife
we can spoil the evil goals
Freedom in a world of love
freedom is the only way
learning to respect each other
is the future of today

aug 22nd, 1998 /march 24th, 2005

Future

will be what we decide it to be

it has all been said and done
we still pretend we havnt heard it
laughable

we rather suffer than take the courage
to stand up to our beliefs,
if we have any left
so we deserve whatever may come
unless we decide to change

our future

why dont you start with yours?

dec 31st, 2003
sep, 23rd 2005

Little Hands

little hands
touching items far too big
little heads
watching movies far too rough
little backs
carrying loads far too heavy
little eyes
seeing things far too tough

little people
with their senses straight and clear
little people
with the make-up of grown ups
grown up people
with their backs all bend and cricked
grown up people
loading their frustration on the kids

let the world turn back to childhood
let the beauty rule our life
let the clearness in the children
teach us how we can survive

dec 31st, 2003

No Silence

Running and a hard time breathing
trying to combine the both
forget eating, restless sleeping
shower and no change of clothes.
Time ??
Wondering why the date is wrong
on my desk tops' timer
clock repeats the pick up song
children wait at diner
Doggon time!!
Frowning over pants too short
didnt they look right some days ago?
Jackets fading colors, fits are overboard,
hair cuts overdue no time to go.
Time??
Socks with holes and shoes too small,
single gloves and missing hats
kids grow into people over fall
argue over make-up sets
Time flies !
Nail polish spots around the sink
the light stays on too long
discussing boy friends with a wink
global interests growing strong.
Time??
a full- time life
need no
time out
to breath
in silence

dec 27th, 2003 /march 24th, 2005

Piece of Sky
(to my mom with all my love)
So many questions are running through my mind
so deep inside, so fearful, so unkind
so many doubts and yet so much to give
knowing there's one life left to live

Where I go, I always seem to reason why
it would remain so much to know,
but times are flying by;
so many questions stayed unheard
it seems so hard to find the words
how to explain how much I care
the fear of you not being there

Go and try
and always search for a piece of sky
what good is life you dont ask why
Go and see
there's always more, yet more to be
it takes all love to set you free !
Did I care
enough of all the ones that I love
I ask myself how could I dare
to ever say I did enough ?
Your guiding hands were leading me
your heart and soul were feading me
despair and darkness and through pain
how could your love remain the same

soundtrack, jan, 1991

Points of View

You said:
I think it is the point of view
and very interesting too
to look at it from laying here
it seems not being so severe

I thought:
that it could rather be
of insignificance to me
a matter of no great concern
but maybe we both need to learn
that sometimes
at a certain point
It's not the view
it is the joint
and yes indeed we have to learn
that is the point of no return

nov 21st, 1998

„... hell is our own creation and the devil is our own distorted image in the mirror of the world. Historically we have preferred sickness to acceptance of this burden of spiritual responsibility..."

Indian Wisdom
Grandfather Little Crow, USA

The Secret of Strength

wisdom fell upon my life
my parents smiles so mild
in their love and education
when I was a child
criticism stroke me hard
misbehaving of a child
love and hate and constant searching
when I was running wild
doubts confused my life a lot
in troubles of lifes' game
ups and downs and backs and forths
when I was still to blame
worries filled my heart
in days of death and birth
spinning in emotions
when I came back to earth
picture frames of past emotions
shapes and colors manifold
showing life's a constant process
when my life turned into gold
stepping out the picture frames
view the contents art
giving it what it deserves
respect for an encouraged heart
I take it now for what it is
a moment in the past
and every breath carries me on
with it the strength will last

dec 26th, 2003

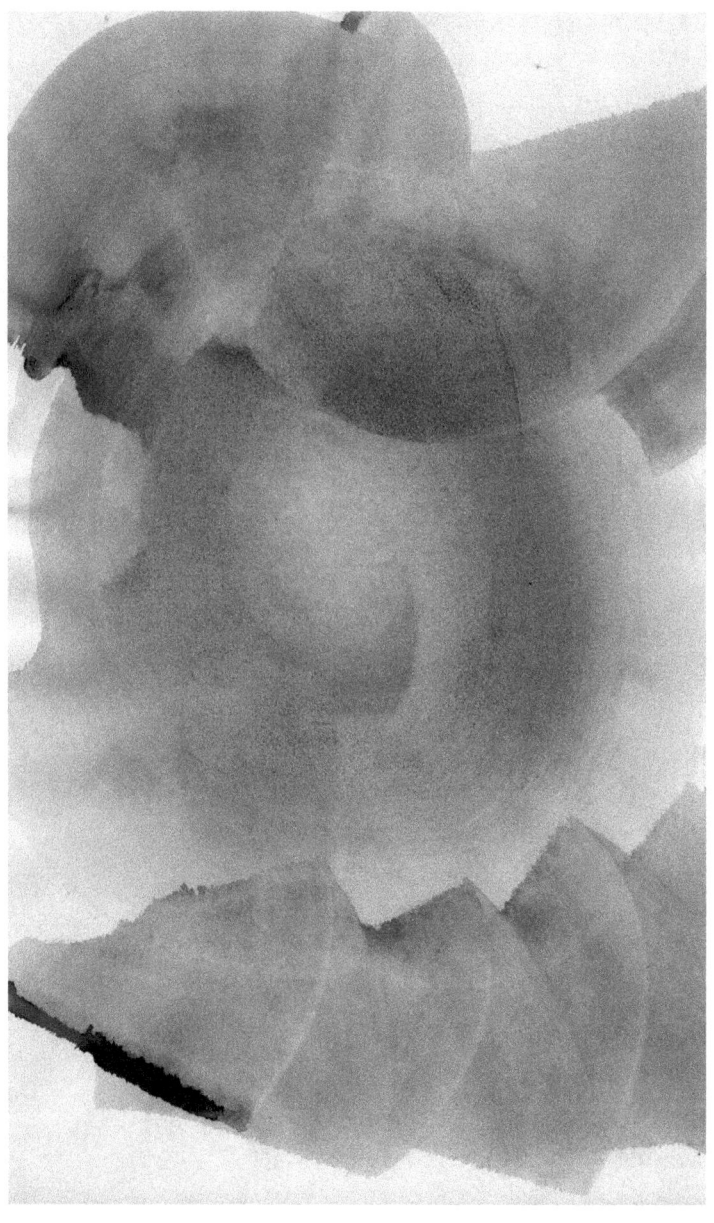

Solid Color
(to 15 years of experience with rassism)

Turn your head and look around
this world is filled with pain
if you are black, if you are white
you go and choose your game
we're split in gangs, we're split in mind
some have the might some are just blind
we waste our time in fuzz' and fights
noone is right or wrong
it's all about: respect the rights
it's not where you belong
we lost our trust, we lost our heart
we need to change for a new start !

SOLID COLOR -- choose where you belong
SOLID COLOR -- united we're strong
It's not the clothes, it's not the race
it's not the color of your hair
it's what you feel, it's what you think
it's if you ever care
you feel the need to live the truth
to break them down- old dusty rules
we need to go and buy ourselves
some glasses all the same
then everyone'd be colorblind
and noone's left to blame
we need to mend our broken heart
we need to change for a new start

(soundtrack, oct 1993)

Unique

Every person is unique
thousands crossed my life so far
have not met the same kind twice
every person is unique

every person's beautiful
deep inside an inner glow
sometimes hidden sometimes free
lights its way through the lifes' show

everybody has a skill
countless possibilties I see
amazing and suprizing me
variations wonderf'lly

have you found your
inner glow, skill and beauty , yet?
have you given up or started
to believe,- trust your facet?

dec 24th, 2003

Who Cares

if you stay or if you go
who'll know where the way will lead
if you breath in or if you blow
who'll care if two ends meet

if you remain
the picture you were raised into
if you contain
all hidden skills you own
if you just strain
through lifes desicions willingly
if you refrain
the million other options

if you stay or if you go
who'll know of all you need
if not yourself, it is just you
who cares if two ends meet

dec 31st, 2003

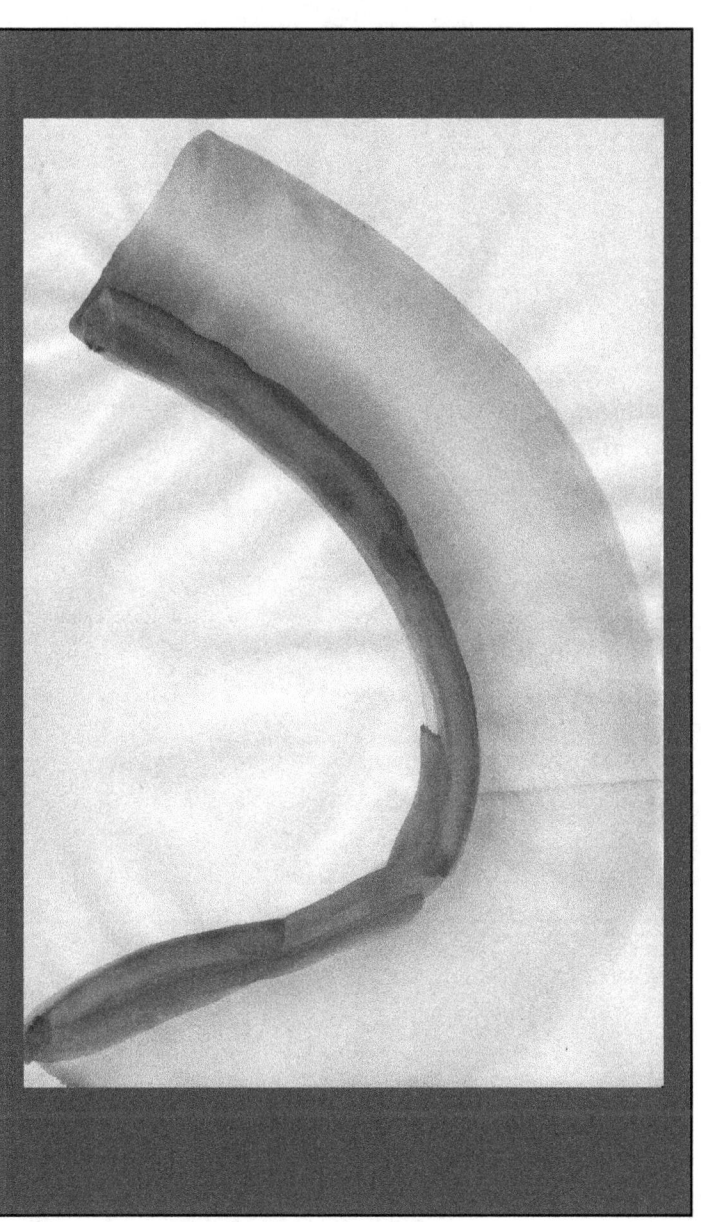

„...all of the nature is in perpetual communication with all of life.."

Indian Wisdom
Grandfather Little Crow, USA

foto©MB by GV 2002

About the author - Biography

Joy C. Green lives and works in Munich, Germany on a constant basis since 1991. She has been travelling and living around the world and her interests, studies and works are multiple. Philosophy and sport, theology and science, music and medicine, hardly any subject stayed untouched. To her master degree in science (biology and chemistry, 1991), she added a degree in pedagogy (1992). Later came an education as a naturopath (1997), specializing in ShenDo-Shiatsu (1999). Intense studies on music, voice production, voice therapy and voice teaching in the USA(1999-2004) followed. Until today she performs live, after she had appeared on stages from Bejing to L.A. as a singer over two thousand times with various bands in different styles in the past since 1981.
Today she works as a vocal teacher, musician, singer, music promoter, composer and shiatsu therapist. She translates, writes and publishes books. Her discography contains over 25 CDs until today. She found her own institute for voice and music education in 2000, GREEN VOICES© and was chairwoman in the institute of ethnomedicine© from 2000-2008.
She is mother of four children.

Munich, Germany in 2013/2020

www.greenvoices.de

Simon Schott's story about Jacob

Jacob cant sleep, he is twisting and turning.
His wife wakes up and asks him about his trouble.
He says: "Oh dear, you know, I owe Mustafa 40.000 silver coins by tomorrow morning, but I dont have the money. What should I do???"

His wifes gets up opens their bedroom window and screams down to Mustafas house:
"Mustafa, wake up, wake up…listen, Jacob doesnt have the 40.000 silver coins and cannot pay you tomorrow morning".
Then she lays back down in bed.

"Now go to sleep, now he knows and you can let him have the sleepless night."

(an old arabian story)

Contents

	PAGE
Introduction	
about LIFE	
pic. Mother earth (Tami+Jenny 2005)	8
Earth, the	10
pic. fire (Phyllis 2005)	11
Fire, the	12
Friendship	13
pic. limo+heals (Tami+Phyllis 2005)	14
Hot Summer City	15
Indian saying	16
Let me be-me	17
Little Things	18
Magic	20
pic. houses (Phyllis 2004)	21
Metal, the	22
Perfection	24/25
pic. tiger (Garance 2004)	23
Schemer, the	26
Solitude	27
pic. symphony (Phyllis 2005)	28
Symphonie of life	29
pic. water (Phyllis 2003)	30
Water, the	31
pic. bird on tree (Phyllis 2005)	32
Wood, the	33
about LOVE	
pic. hearts (Tami+Jenny 2002)	35
As long as I have you	36
Dont	37
Fly	38
pic. heart daddy (Jen 2005)	39
Just love	40
Keep on going	41
Miss	42
pic. flowertree (Jenny 2003)	43
No love to give	44
pic. shades of love (Jenny 2005)	45

Power of love, the	46
pic. sandstorm (Phyllis 2004)	47
Touch	48
pic. touch (Jenny 2005)	49
Sometimes	50
Would you mind	51
pic. lips (Jenny,Tami,Phyllis 2005)	52
Your lips	53

about HOPE & FUTURE

pic. dino (Tami 2005)	55
Best years of our life	56
pic. cross-roads (Phyllis 2005)	57
Circle of searching	58
pic. dolphin (Garance 2004)	59
Destination	60
pic. music note (Jenny 2004)	61
Distinction	62
pic. dragon (Phyllis 2004)	63
Freedom	64
Future, the	65
Little hands	66
pic. color flower (Jenny 2004)	67
No silence	68
Piece of sky	69
Points of view	70
Indian wisdom	71
pic. horse (Garance 2003)	72
Secret of strength, the	73
pic. color (Tami 2004)	74
Solid color	75
pic. bird (Phyllis 2005)	76
Unique	77
pic. new years (Tami 2004)	78
Who cares	79
pic. rainbow (Jenny 2004)	80
Indian wisdom	81
picture & biography author	82/83
Simon Schott's Story about Jacob	84

CPSIA information can be obtained
at www.ICGtesting.com
Printed in the USA
LVHW040942281122
733859LV00018B/1862